Brooklyn Park Elem.

52074745

$12.95

List

PARTNERS

# MATTHEW HENSON & ROBERT PEARY
## THE RACE FOR THE NORTH POLE

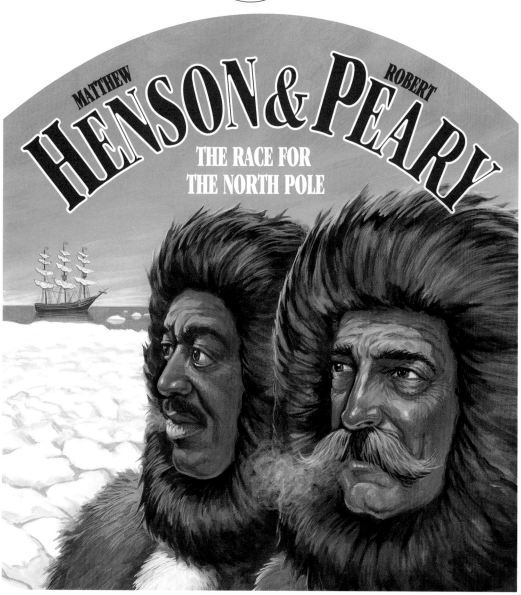

BY

Laurie Rozakis

Illustrations by Tom Foty

A BLACKBIRCH PRESS BOOK

WOODBRIDGE, CONNECTICUT

Published by Blackbirch Press, Inc.
One Bradley Road
Woodbridge , CT 06525

©1994 Blackbirch Press, Inc.
First Edition

Printed in Hong Kong

10 9 8 7 6 5 4 3 2 1

**Library of Congress Cataloging-in-Publication Data**

Rozakis, Laurie.
    Matthew Henson & Robert Peary: the race for the North Pole / by
Laurie Rozakis —1st ed.
        p.   cm. — (Partners)
    Includes bibliographical references and index.
    ISBN 1-56711-066-5
    1. Peary, Robert E. (Robert Edwin), 1856–1920—Juvenile literature.
2. Henson, Matthew Alexander, 1866–1955—Juvenile literature. 3. Afro-
American explorers—Biography—Juvenile literature. 4. Explorers—United
States—Biography—Juvenile literature. 5. North Pole—Discovery and explo-
ration—Juvenile literature. [1. Peary, Robert E. (Robert Edwin), 1856–1920.
2. Henson, Matthew Alexander, 1866–1955. 3. Explorers. 4. Afro-
Americans—Biography. 5. North Pole—Discovery and exploration.] I. Title.
II. Title: Matthew Henson and Robert Peary. III. Title: Henson and Peary.
IV. Series.
G635.P4R69  1994
919.8'04—dc20                           93-43384
[B]                                             CIP

# ▪ ▪ ▪ Contents ▪ ▪ ▪

The incredible journey of Matthew Henson and Robert Peary took them through a harsh, frozen wasteland.

# 1

# On the Roof of the World

ar, far north on the Earth, a small band of men struggled against icy blasts of wind. The howling Arctic gales drove needles of ice into their faces. The bitter east wind was like a sharp sword, slicing right through their thick fur parkas.

It was 60 degrees below zero. If the men spilled a cup of hot tea, it would vanish before it hit the ground. The extreme cold turned the water into tiny crystals of ice, too small to see. It was so cold that the men's noses, cheeks, and toes turned black with frostbite. Their brandy was frozen solid. Even their petroleum jelly was hard and white. But these men were determined to complete their journey. Robert

**The North Pole is known as the "roof of the world" and is the most northern spot on the map.**

Peary and Matthew Henson were going to be the first to reach the North Pole—or die trying.

In 1909, no one had been to the North Pole. It is in the Arctic Ocean, somewhere on the ice. People call it the "roof of the world" because it is located at the top of the Earth. If you are standing at the North Pole, the only way you can turn is south.

## An Eerie Land

That far north, night and day are very different from other places. In the Arctic, it is dark for six months and light for six months. The explorers could not cross the ice in the dark. But if they waited too long to leave, the summer sun would melt miles of ice before they could cross it coming back. They would be stranded on chunks of ice or plunge into the freezing water of the Arctic Ocean.

*Robert Peary and Matthew Henson had tried to reach the North Pole twice before.*

Peary and Henson had tried to reach the North Pole twice before. Both times they had been beaten by brutal blasts of wind, towering blocks of ice, and starvation. Could they make it this time? There would not be another chance.

## Racing Against the Sun

Matthew Henson, leading the group, cracked his whip above his dogs' ears. "Huk! Huk!" he shouted, and they were off across the frozen sea. But traveling this region was not easy, partly because the Arctic ice is not smooth. There are great mountains of salty *swells*, which are gleaming chunks of blue-and-white ice. These swells look like huge boulders thrown into a pile. The men had to hack through the hills of ice in order to move forward. They carried their supplies on *sledges*, which are long, heavy sleds with wooden runners that are pulled by teams of dogs. The dogs, like huskies, were more wolf than dog. They have thick coats of fur because they were born and raised in the bitter Arctic cold.

The men pushed the sledges while the dogs strained against their harness. Matthew Henson cracked the whip hard, but even the powerful dogs could not push through the solid ice. Suddenly, they came to a patch of snow, but it was just as hard to move on as ice. The men and dogs quickly sank into the snow up to their necks. And then came another danger.

The pull of the moon's gravity and the movement of the Earth often crack the ice in the Arctic and create lanes of water called *leads.* These leads could open at any moment, plunging the men into the swirling icy water. The explorers had to act fast if they were going to avoid disaster. With great skill and cooperation, the team managed to pull itself out of the snow and move on. But this would not be the last danger they would face.

When Matthew Henson fell through the ice, Ootah bravely rescued him from the freezing waters.

## So Near . . . But So Far

On April 1, 1909, Peary and Henson were about 135 miles from their goal. They had 40 strong dogs, 4 of the bravest *Inuits* (native people) in all the Arctic (Ootah, Egingwah, Seegloo, and Ooqueah), and a snowy wilderness lit by a sun that never sets. At midnight they set off and marched for ten hours. The weather was calm and everyone was cheerful. It seemed as if nothing could go wrong.

On April 3, they came to a lead covered with fresh, thin ice. As Matthew Henson pushed his sledge over it, the runner broke through. The ice ripped open, and Matthew plunged into the freezing Arctic Ocean! Ootah raced over and quickly but carefully yanked the fallen explorer out by his hood. Matthew lay huddled on the ice, gasping for breath. He stripped off his wet boots and pounded the water out of his fur before it froze solid to his body. As he struggled to his feet, the other men got ready to make the final push to the Pole. Would they make it? No one knew.

How did these men wind up on this amazing adventure? The story begins many years ago, with the birth of a boy named Robert Peary.

# 2

# Robert Peary

obert Edwin Peary was born May 6, 1856, in Pennsylvania's Allegheny Mountains. Little "Bertie" was not even three years old when his father died. At that point, his mother packed up her red-haired, blue-eyed son and rejoined her family in Maine.

## Mama's Boy

Back in Maine, Mrs. Peary spent all her time with her young son, teaching him about birds, flowers, fish, and trees. They often walked along the Atlantic shore and hunted for shells and birds' eggs together. Bertie was a generally happy child until he entered school when he was seven years old. Each day, Mary Peary made Bertie wear a sunbonnet to protect his fair skin. Although he was unhappy, Bertie

11

When Robert Peary was seven years old, his mother made him wear a sunbonnet to school each morning.

would not disobey his mother. "What a sissy!" the other boys teased. "You're nothing but a mama's boy!" No one would ever play with him. Without friends, Bertie spent all his free time alone. He spent most of his time making big collections of shells, birds' eggs, and pressed flowers.

12

## A Loner

When Bertie was ten years old, he took up *taxidermy.* Taxidermy is preserving and stuffing the skins of dead animals and posing them in life-like ways. Mrs. Peary was pleased that he was so interested in nature, but she wanted him to have friends, too. She decided to send him to a boarding school. But, even there, Bertie made no friends. Soon he had a room all by himself.

Mrs. Peary then thought of another way to help her son. When Bertie enrolled in high school, she bought a house in Portland, Maine. She set up a large room where her son could bring all his friends, and she baked lots of cookies. But Bertie just hung a "busy" sign on his door and stayed in his room.

When Bertie was in the tenth grade, Mrs. Peary spoke to a doctor about her son's lonely ways. He told her it was time for Bertie to get away from her for awhile. So Mrs. Peary sent Bertie south to tour the country for three months. When he returned from his travels, he had changed. Now, he seemed more like a self-confident young man. As soon as he passed his final exams at school, Bertie set up a shop as a taxidermist.

## A Good Business

Bertie's taxidermy business was a big success. Many women bought large, colorful birds to display in their homes. And they bought small birds to wear on their hats—which was very fashionable in the late 1800s. Hunters were also eager to preserve what they had shot. And many museums liked the life-like way that Bertie posed animals.

**After high school, Bertie opened a successful taxidermy business.**

The boys in town soon decided that shy young Bertie was worth knowing.  He was not only a talented taxidermist, he was also a star athlete.  He could dive, skate, and swim like a champ.  But Bertie was still a loner.  He most enjoyed hunting and fishing by himself and exploring Maine's coast.  One lonely spot touched his heart, and he called it Eagle Island.  Later he built a home there.

## College Days

After working in his business for a while, Bertie was ready for college.  His mother had already decided that he was going to attend Bowdoin College in Maine.  And as usual, the obedient Bertie went along with his mother's wishes—he even won a scholarship to Bowdoin!  But Mrs. Peary was not yet ready to let go of her son.  "I am going to college with you!" she announced.  She rented rooms near the college, and, for two years, Bertie lived with his mother rather than with his classmates.

Bertie was respected at college for his athletic skills, keen mind, and determination.  But he was not well liked.  Bertie, however, did not really care what others thought of him.

After graduating in 1877, he set up an office as a *surveyor.* A surveyor is someone who plots out and documents sections of land. Unfortunately, Bertie was less successful as a surveyor than he had been doing taxidermy. As he grew older, he also began to understand that he was not generally well liked. "I should like to gain that attractive personality that when I was with a person they would have to like me whether they wanted to or not," he wrote in his diary at that time. He also desired fame. "I would like to acquire a name . . . which would make me feel that I was the peer of anyone I might meet."

## Nothing Seemed Impossible

As he matured, Bertie began to see that he had no future in a small town in Maine. When he was 22 years old, he applied for a job as a draftsman in Washington, D.C. In January of 1880, he was offered the job, at $10 a week.

The tall, young bachelor soon got into the swing of the Washington social world. He enjoyed dancing and going out on the town. Among the young ladies that he dated was Josephine Diebitsch, the daughter of a Smithsonian Institution scholar. Bertie

In 1880, Bertie took a job as a draftsman in a
Washington, D.C., office.

found Josephine's charm and intelligence appealing. On August 11, 1888, three years after they met, Bertie and Josephine were married.

During this time, Washington was buzzing with talk about creating a canal between the Atlantic and Pacific oceans. Bertie thought that this could be his ticket to fame. But Mrs. Peary did not want her son to travel to Panama. She convinced him to wait.

### "You're in the Navy Now!"

For nearly a year, Bertie worked at his boring draftsman job. Then he saw a notice for a position in the Civil Engineer Corps of the U.S. Navy and took the ten-day test. Only 4 of the 200 men who applied were accepted, and Bertie was one of the lucky ones. As a start, he was given the rank of lieutenant.

Bertie's first job was to inspect a pier in Key West, Florida. After he dove into the harbor and examined it, he wrote a new plan for the pier. Then he did the job himself, at a cost of $6,000. The Navy had estimated it would cost $60,000!

His overjoyed bosses decided to give him an even greater challenge—one that would soon lead him to the most important meeting of his life.

# 3

# Matthew Henson

On a spring day in Washington, D.C., in 1887, Robert Peary was getting ready to survey Nicaragua, a tropical country in Central America. His job was to find the best place to dig a canal through Nicaragua's jungle that would link the Atlantic and Pacific oceans. That morning, Robert set off to get a hat to protect his head from the blazing tropical sun. He wound up at B.H. Steinmetz and Sons, Hatters.

Inside the store, Robert asked Mr. Steinmetz for a sun helmet. While he was waiting, he mentioned to Steinmetz that he was looking for an assistant. The store owner thought a moment and said, "My clerk, Matthew Henson, might want the job. He is a hard worker, and someone you can depend on." Just then, a young black man came from the back room with Peary's hat. It was Matthew Henson.

## Terror in the South

Matthew Alexander Henson was born on August 8, 1866, on his parents' farm in Maryland—only one year after the Civil War ended. Unlike most of their friends, Matthew's parents had never been slaves. But, like many other African Americans living in the South at the time, the Hensons were attacked by the Ku Klux Klan and other groups who did not want to

**Because they were African Americans, Matthew Henson's family suffered from prejudice and attacks by the Ku Klux Klan in the 1860s.**

see blacks vote or attend public school. To escape from the racial violence, the Hensons sold their farm and moved to Washington, D.C.

When Matthew was seven years old, his mother died and his father sent him to stay with his uncle, who lived in the area. There, Matthew went to school for the next six years. When he was 13 years old, Matthew's father died and his uncle could no longer care for him. To support himself, Matthew worked as a waiter in a nearby Washington, D.C., restaurant. The restaurant's owner let him sleep in the kitchen and eat leftover food. Matthew was warm and fed, but he wanted adventure.

## An Able-Bodied Seaman

Matthew decided that working on a ship would be more exciting. In the fall of 1879, he walked 40 miles to Baltimore's harbor, went up to the silver-haired Captain Childs of the *Katie Hines,* and asked for a job. The captain was so impressed with Matthew that he hired him immediately. For the next five years, Matthew cleaned Captain Childs's room, served his meals, washed his dishes, and helped the cook. The men on the ship liked the hard-working young man. They taught him how to repair engines, navigate by the stars, and build almost anything. The captain liked Matthew so much that he taught him geography, history, mathematics, and lent him books. "These books are the beginning," Captain Childs told Matthew. "Make them your fists."

Matthew sailed from China to Japan to the Philippines. He sailed across the Atlantic Ocean to France, Africa, and southern Russia. He even sailed through the Arctic. And all the time, he continued to learn. When Matthew was 19, Captain Childs died and was buried at sea. Heartbroken, Matthew returned to Baltimore.

## The Meeting of a Lifetime

Matthew tried to find work in Baltimore, but there were not many opportunities for black people in 1885. The young man soon discovered that people didn't care about his skills and learning—only his color. He worked as a driver, a bellhop, a messenger, and a night watchman. Soon, he decided to go to Washington, D.C., where he got a job as a clerk in the Steinmetz and Sons hat shop.

Matthew and Robert first met in a Washington, D.C., hat shop in 1887.

Matthew Henson and Robert Peary looked at each other across the counter on that day they met in 1887. Matthew saw a tall, red-haired man with steely, blue-gray eyes. Robert saw a steady, calm, honest young man. Even though Matthew was only 20 years old, he had already traveled around the world. Robert decided to ask Matthew to be his helper in Nicaragua. "Sir, I'd like that job very much," Matthew answered.

23

Their first project together was sort of a funny way for these men to begin a partnership. Matthew Henson and Robert Peary, who would later make history by being the first people to reach the North Pole, first had to travel in the opposite direction—to the jungle!

In November 1887, Matthew sailed with 45 U.S. engineers and 100 black Jamaican workers to Nicaragua. As Robert's servant, Matthew cooked and cleaned while the engineers measured and the workers chopped through the jungle. Soon, however, Robert recognized Matthew's intelligence and skill and gave him more important and demanding work.

## The First Greenland Expedition

After seven months, the Nicaragua survey was done. As the men sailed back to New York, Robert asked Matthew to come with him as he tried to cross Greenland, a snowy country just below the North Pole. Matthew quickly agreed. In June of 1891, the Greenland expedition set off. Their tiny ship, the *Kite,* was packed with many kinds of food, including *pemmican*—a beef, fat, and raisin mixture that explorers eat for energy. There were also skis and

snowshoes, guns and bullets, sledges, woolen clothing, a stove, pots and pans, cameras, and a hundred
tons of coal.

Robert planned to become famous by being the
first person to cross Greenland. The country's name,
however, did not tell the truth about the country:
"Greenland" is mostly covered in ice. Robert wanted to cross the southern end, which is the shortest
route to travel—but also the most dangerous.

As they set off toward Greenland, the *Kite* sailed
past towering white glaciers and struggled
through cracks in the stubborn, rugged ice.
The little ship finally dropped anchor in
McCormick Bay, Greenland. On August 8—
Matthew's birthday—he had the first party of
his life. Matthew's wife (who joined them on
the ship) cooked mock turtle soup, stew of
*auk* (a little bird), green peas, eider duck, corn,
tomatoes, and apricot pie. The food was so deli-
cious that Matthew remembered this party for the
rest of his life.

*In June 1891, the expedition to Greenland set off.*

Soon after they dropped anchor, the explorers set
out to meet the local Inuit. They hoped the men
would help them hunt polar bears, seals, walruses,

reindeer, caribou, and foxes for meat and fur. They also hoped the Inuit women would take the animal hides and sew them into warm clothing.

On August 18, four Inuit men walked into camp. They stepped close to Matthew, pointed to his skin, and said, "Inuit! Inuit!" They thought that Matthew was an Inuit who had just returned to his homeland. From that moment on, the Inuit called Matthew "Miy Paluk," which means "dear little Matthew." They taught him how to speak the Inuit language, to eat meat raw and bloody, and to drive a dog sledge with a 30-foot sealskin whip. Matthew even learned to build a snow igloo with 50 blocks of snow in just an hour. These basic skills would be very important to Matthew in the future. They would help him and his fellow explorers survive in the dangerous and harsh frozen world they were about to explore. But even though Matthew knew the most about surviving in the Arctic, Robert picked another man from the camp to travel with him on this historic journey across Greenland.

On September 24, 1892, the first North Greenland Expedition returned home and Robert was a hero. Matthew, however, was barely noticed.

# ...4...

# **Reaching the Pole**

The never-ending sea ice of the Arctic piles into mountains that reach high into the sky. Under your feet, the ice moves and cracks without warning. One false step and you may plunge into the water, never to come out. The swirling black ocean is cold, dark, and deadly. With all these dangers, no wonder few people have ever reached the North Pole!

The Inuit knew well how dangerous the Arctic Ocean could be. They believed the ocean held a fierce devil, called *Tornasuk*, the spirit of the frozen sea. The ocean was dangerous because Tornasuk could drag people to their death. But the North Pole had an even more cruel devil they called *Kokoyah*. They believed that only the bravest person would venture near the North Pole.

27

## Trying for the North Pole

On June 26, 1893, Robert, Matthew, and a crew of ten took off for the frozen north again. This time Matthew was sure that he would be chosen as one of the men to trek with Robert to the North Pole. But once again, Robert picked others to accompany him, and Matthew was left back at camp.

Unlike their first trip, this expedition was a failure. The men could only go 128 miles before the dogs went mad or froze to death in the ice storms. When they returned to camp, all of Robert's men wanted to go home—all except for one: Matthew Henson. Robert was only able to talk one other man, Hugh Lee, into staying. On April 1, 1895, the three men set out for the North Pole again.

## "A Long Race with Death"

It was warm for the north Arctic, only 14 degrees below zero! It was sunny, too, and the flat fields of ice were so shiny that it hurt to look at them. The three men traveled to where Robert had left a giant pile of supplies, but everything was buried in the snow. "We'll go on anyway," Robert said, "we have enough walrus meat." The others agreed.

Eating the walrus meat, however, would not be easy. When they tried to bite into the meat, it was frozen so hard that it cut the inside of their mouths like glass. They tried to warm it in their tea, but the slippery, raw, red chunks looked too bloody to eat. Lacking enough food, they got weaker and weaker.

Finally, the men found a herd of walrus, and Matthew shot one just as it charged toward Robert. The three starving explorers gobbled the warm, bloody meat and threw chunks to their skinny dogs. With their stomachs filled, the men marched on. They made it as far as Independence Bay, but they could go no further. Towering cliffs that could not be crossed were now in their way. On June 1, bitterly disappointed, they trudged back to camp. Years later Matthew called the trip back to camp "a long race with death."

The men had eaten so little nourishing food that their teeth had started to fall out. Upon returning, only Matthew was brave enough to do what the Inuits told him: He drank bowls and bowls of seals' blood. Sure enough, he recovered first.

On August 3, 1895, the three men returned to Washington, D.C. Robert had to have something to

On their third expedition, Matthew shot a walrus just as it charged toward Robert. The men and their hungry dogs then feasted on the warm meat.

show for his two years in Greenland, so he brought
two huge meteorites he had found.  Today, visitors
can see these meteorites at the Museum of Natural
History in New York City.

## Tragedy Strikes

On July 4, 1898, Robert and Matthew set off again
for the North Pole.  This time, however, their ship
got trapped in the ice 700 miles from their
goal.  Robert became frantic when he found
out that a brave Norwegian explorer named
Sverdrup was also heading for the Pole.  He
knew if their ship was stuck, Sverdrup
would beat them to the goal!  Robert decided to march through the long Arctic night
no matter what the cost.  Robert, Matthew,
and their expedition finally made it to a
stopping point—Fort Conger—and they were
ahead of Sverdrup.  But their journey had taken a
terrible toll.  Robert's toes had frozen solid.  A fierce
storm then trapped the men in their cabin.  Matthew
cared for Robert until the storm let up.  Finally, on
February 18, Matthew strapped Robert to a sledge
and set off to return to the ship.  There, all but two

> *Their journeys across the frozen land were brutal and dangerous.  On one trip, Robert's toes had frozen solid.*

Large chunks of ice would break apart as the explorers journeyed across the Arctic. On one trip, the men were stranded on an ice floe for hours.

of Robert's toes had to be *amputated* (cut off). For the rest of his life, he would have difficulty walking.

On April 6, 1902, Robert, Matthew, and four Inuit helpers once again stepped onto the frozen Arctic ice. Matthew saw once more why the Inuit so feared the region. The ice split apart and jammed with fearsome roars. As it split, *floes,* or islands of ice, were created. The men tried jumping from ice floe to ice floe, but too often they got stranded on a chunk of ice, and then they had to wait until new ice formed. With Robert still weak from his foot prob-lems, Matthew led the way. He searched in vain for a better way through the treacherous ice but could not avoid the punishment of the Arctic.

*On April 21, 1902, the men ran out of food and could go no further.*

On April 21, the men ran out of food and could go no further. They had reached the point 84' 16" north latitude—which was the American record for the farthest north ever traveled—but it was still not the Pole. Disappointed and tired, the expedition returned home. More than three years would pass before Robert and Matthew would feel prepared to face the challenges of the Arctic again.

## Accomplishing the Impossible

On July 16, 1905, Matthew and Robert sailed north again with three assistants. As they traveled up the coast of Greenland, they took on 33 Inuit families, 200 dogs, and tons of whale and walrus meat. The ship stank with meat, dogs, and unwashed people.

Humbled by his past attempts, Robert now made a new plan. One group would find the best route and make a trail. Five small groups then would follow and every 50 to 75 miles, one of the five

**When Robert's toes froze solid during an expedition in February 1898, Matthew had to strap him to a sledge and bring him back to the ship.**

groups would go back with the weakest dogs. This would save the food for the strongest.

On March 1, Matthew and his team of Inuits left to try once again to blaze a trail to the Pole. By April 21, they were only 175 miles from the Pole, but they were out of food and were forced to eat their dogs. By the time they arrived back at their ship, only two dogs were left. They had set a new world record, but they still had not reached the Pole.

35

## Victory at Last!

Robert now knew that he would not have too many more chances to reach the Pole. He was nearly 50 years old, and time and money had nearly run out. On July 6, 1908, Robert once again loaded a ship. He picked the six strongest and bravest men he could find, and again all the men marched in teams. But this time, Robert knew enough to ask Matthew to come with him to the Pole.

By April 5, they were only one day's march from their goal. The next day, on April 6, Robert took a reading. At first he couldn't believe what he saw. His reading showed 90 degrees north! They had made it! "We will plant the Stars and Stripes at the North Pole," he shouted. The men gave three cheers and took pictures of themselves with the flag. They also dreamed of what a bright future they would all have. But even though their journey was over, their troubles were not.

On April 6, 1909, Matthew Henson and Robert Peary finally made it to the North Pole and accomplished their lifelong dream.

# ...∎5∎...

# After the Pole

Matthew and Robert did not reach a radio station until September 5, five months after they left the North Pole. It was then that Robert sent news of his success to his wife. "Have made good at last," he radioed. "I have the Pole!"

On August 17, 1909, Robert learned that Dr. Frederick A. Cook, another explorer, claimed that he had reached the North Pole first. "Peary was never even close," said the Inuits who had been with Dr. Cook. "We simply laughed at it," Matthew and Robert replied. But Cook was not playing a joke.

38

Worse than that, most people believed his claim. Days later, when Robert and Matthew landed in Newfoundland, they learned that the Royal Danish Geographical Society had already accepted Cook's claim—and awarded him a gold medal! Robert and Matthew had struggled 18 years to reach the North Pole, and now the world thought they were fakes.

## Personalities Clash

Robert was so angry at what had happened that he became very distant and unfriendly. To the public, Cook was a charming, easygoing man; Robert was as cold and bitter as the Arctic itself. Cook told riveting tales about the danger he faced getting to the Pole; Robert gave a dull list of details. Cook earned thousands of dollars talking about his adventure; Robert was so hurt that he would not talk at all. He finally went home to Maine to wait until the scientific proof he brought back showed that he was telling the truth.

Matthew, however, decided to take a stand and tell people the truth. He gave many stirring public speeches. He also wrote about their discovery in a book he called *A Negro Explorer at the North Pole.*

## The Forgotten Hero

By December 15, the National Geographic Society ruled that Robert Peary and Matthew Henson *had* reached the Pole first. Robert got a gold medal. And a captain known as Bartlett—one of the men on the expedition—also got a medal. But Matthew Henson got nothing. He was not even included in the report. The Navy also wanted to promote Robert to the rank of rear admiral, but first they had a few questions.

"Why did you take a black man to the North Pole with you?" they asked. Robert did not tell them the truth. He did not say that he owed his life to Matthew Henson and that without him, he never could have reached the Pole. Instead, he said the reason was because Matthew could not get home without a white man leading him. But the other men on the trip knew the truth. "Matthew Henson went to the Pole with Peary because he was a better man than any one of us," one man from the trip wrote. For many years after his promotion, Robert would not speak to Matthew, and the two men grew far apart.

*"Matthew Henson was a better man than any of us," one expedition member wrote.*

Today, we live in a country where people of many different backgrounds live side by side.  But this was not the case in 1909.  In America, blacks and whites were most often officially separated.  And whites did not treat blacks as their equals.  When Robert and Matthew were in the Arctic, they shared the same chunk of frozen walrus;  back in the United States, they were not allowed to sit at the same table.  In the Arctic, they slept in the same igloo;  back in the United States, there were separate hotels for blacks and whites.  Black people were not even allowed to drink from the same water fountain as white people.  On their trip, Robert and Matthew reached the North Pole together.  Back in the United States, Matthew was not given proper credit as Robert's true partner.  Because of the way blacks were treated, Matthew was only considered Robert's "faithful colored servant."  Matthew and some of the others on the trip knew that this attitude was wrong, but many other people did not.

The white world ignored Matthew Henson's victory, but the black world honored him.  In 1909, the Colored Commercial Association of Chicago gave

Matthew Henson a gold medal. And black people in New York City held a big dinner in his honor and gave him a gold watch.

Despite these honors, Matthew could only find work as a parking garage attendant in Brooklyn, New York, where he earned $16 a week. When he was 46 years old, he got a job as a customshouse clerk where he made $900 a year. He worked at the customshouse until he was 70 years old and retired on a small pension.

When Robert lay dying in 1920, he called for Matthew. His fellow explorer came, and the two men had one last talk together. Before he died, Robert asked Matthew to forgive him for not telling the truth to the world. He also admitted that he owed his life to Matthew and that, if it hadn't been for Matthew, the group would never have made it to the North Pole at all.

## Credit Long Overdue

It was not until many years after Robert's death that Matthew was rewarded for his accomplishment. In 1937, he was invited to join the Explorers' Club, which was a very select group. The next year he

**Matthew Henson was not officially honored for his achievements until 1944, when the U.S. Congress awarded him with a medal.**

was made an honorary member of the Academy of Science and Art in Pittsburgh, Pennsylvania. In 1938, one of the explorers on the trip to the North Pole asked Congress to honor Matthew Henson, but his efforts were unsuccessful. It was not until 1944 that the U.S. Congress gave Matthew a medal for his "outstanding service to the Government of the United States...for exceptional fortitude, superb seamanship, and fearless determination."

43

## Part of History

Matthew Henson died in 1955. In 1961, the state of Maryland honored him with a plaque in the State House. It reads: "Matthew Alexander Henson, Co-Discoverer of the North Pole with Admiral Robert Edwin Peary, April 6, 1909...exemplification of courage, fortitude, and patriotism."

It took the world a long time to recognize the true partnership between Matthew Henson and Robert Peary. But their achievement was truly a special act of teamwork. Without Matthew Henson's survival skills and navigation abilities, the group would surely not have succeeded. Without Robert Peary's leadership and persistence, the others would have lacked the drive to try and try until they reached their goal. And without the special dream and the bold courage that both Matthew and Robert shared, someone else's name would have gone down in the history books as the first to reach the "roof of the world."

# Chronology

**May 6, 1856**  Robert Edwin Peary born

**August 8, 1866**  Matthew Henson born

**1887**  Robert and Matthew travel to Nicaragua

**1891**  First trip to Greenland

**1893–1895**  Second trip to Greenland

**1896–1897**  Robert and Matthew locate the meteorites

**1898–1902**  Arctic trip

**1905–1906**  Robert and Matthew travel within 175 miles of the North Pole

**April 6, 1909**  Robert and Matthew reach the North Pole

**February 20, 1920**  Robert Peary dies

**March 9, 1955**  Matthew Henson dies

# Glossary

**amputate**   To cut off surgically.

**auk**  A small, oceanic bird found mostly in the Arctic.

**expedition**  Journey of exploration.

**floe**  An island of ice that drifts.

**Inuit**  Native Americans who live in the Arctic region.  The word means "the real people."

**leads**  Lanes of water created by cracks in the ice.

**North Pole**  The most northern point on Earth; the end of the Earth's axis of rotation.

**pemmican**  A mixture of beef, fat, and raisins that is eaten for energy.

**sledge**  A huge sled pulled by dogs over ice and snow.

**surveyor**  A person who plots out and documents sections of land.

**swell**  Large chunk of blue-and-white ice.

**taxidermy**  Preserving animal skins in life-like poses.

# Further Reading

Anderson, Madelyn Klein. *Robert E. Peary and the Fight for the North Pole.* New York: Franklin Watts, 1992.

Angell, Pauline K. *To the Top of the World.* New York: Rand McNally, 1964.

Dolan, Edward F. *Matthew Henson, Black Explorer.* New York: Dodd, Mead, 1979.

Gilman, Michael. *Matthew Henson.* New York: Chelsea House Publishers, 1988.

Weems, John Edward. *Race for the Pole.* New York: Henry Holt, 1960.

# Index